Help the Environment

Saving Water

Charlotte Guillain

Heinemann Library
Chicago Illinois

Picture research: Erica Martin, Hannah Taylor and Ginny Stroud-Lewis
Designed by Philippa Jenkins
Printed and bound in China by South China Printing Company.
12 11 10 09 08
10 9 8 7 6 5 4 3 2 1

Library of Congress Cataloging-in-Publication Data
Guillain, Charlotte.
  Saving water / Charlotte Guillain.
    p. cm. -- (Help the environment)
  Includes bibliographical references and index.
  ISBN-13: 978-1-4329-0886-7 (hc)
  ISBN-13: 978-1-4329-0892-8 (pb)
  1. Water conservation--Juvenile literature. I. Title.
  TD495.G85 2008
  333.91'16--dc22
                        2007041175

Acknowledgments
The publishers would like to thank the following for permission to reproduce photographs: ©Alamy pp. **16** (Bjanka Kadic), **4 bottom left** (Kevin Foy), **17** (Keith M Law), **4 top right**, **23** (Westend 61); ©ardea.com pp. **19** (Jean Michel Labat), **15** (Mark Boulton); ©Brand X Pixtures pp. **4 bottom right**, **21** (Morey Milbradt); ©Corbis pp. **8**, **10** (Randy Faris), **9**, **12** (zefa, Grace); ©Digital Vision p. **4 top left**; ©Getty Images pp. **14** (AFP, Liu Jin, Staff), **13** (medioImages); ©Jupiter Images p. **22** (Polka Dot Images); ©Photoeditinc. p. **5** (Michael Newman); ©Photolibrary pp. **7** (Botanica), **11** (Image 100), **18** (Photoalto), **20** (Radius Images), **6** (Photodisc)

Cover photograph of tap reproduced with permission of ©Fancy (Punchstock). Back cover photograph of a boy washing up reproduced with permission of ©Corbis (zefa, Grace).

Every effort has been made to contact copyright holders of any material reproduced in this book.
Any omissions will be rectified in subsequent printings if notice is given to the publishers.

Contents

What Is the Environment?

The environment is the world all around us.

We need to care for
the environment.

How Do We Use Water?

We use water for many things.

When we save water, we
help the environment.

Ways to Save Water

We use water to wash dishes.

We save water if we turn off the
tap while we wash.
We help the environment.

We use water to clean our teeth.

We save water if we turn off the
tap while we brush.
We help the environment.

We use water to wash our body.

We save water when we take a
shower instead of a bath.
We help the environment.

We waste water if a tap is dripping.

We save water when we turn
off a dripping tap.
We help the environment.

Plants need water to grow.

catches rainwater

We save water by catching
rainwater to water plants.
We help the environment.

17

A hose uses lots of water.

We save water when we use a
watering can instead of a hose.
We help the environment.

We can save water.

We can help the environment.

21

How Are They Helping?

How is this child saving water?

Answer on p. 24

Picture Glossary

environment the world around us

Index

Answer to question on p.22: He is washing a car using a bucket of water instead of a hose.

Note to Parents and Teachers

Before reading
Talk to children about all the ways we use water (drinking, washing, eating, growing things, etc.). Explain that in many places in the world, people do not have clean water that comes out of a tap in their houses. We need to save water and not waste it.

After reading
• Draw a cross-section of a house and divide it into rooms upstairs and downstairs. Label each room: bathroom, bedroom, kitchen, living room. Ask children to think of ways they can save water in each room (e.g. bathroom - turning off the tap while brushing teeth).